Enterprise Agility with OKRs

ADITI AGARWAL

Published By: Aditi Agarwal Books LLC
Date of Publication: July 2019
Language: English

FREE *Membership to the Agile and Lean Leaders Mentoring Network (ALLMN)*

Be a mentor, or learn from experienced Agile and Lean leaders by subscribing to the exclusive Agile and Lean Leaders Facebook Network for Free:

Join the Facebook Group:

https://www.facebook.com/ groups/AgileLeanLeaders/

Subscribe to the **FREE** monthly newsletter on agility and lean thinking and stay in the know!

Get an email digest of trending articles including my recent blogs to your inbox every month.

Subscribe by visiting:

https://mailchi.mp/2c566ed 9e15c/newsletter

To God for his blessings
To my family for their loving support

Table of Contents

Introduction

Enterprise Agility isn't just another buzzword these days. It represents a core capability that an enterprise must have to sustain business and drive outcomes in this fast-paced, competitive, and rapidly changing environment.

This book, enriched with inspiring quotes and insights, shows concrete steps that an enterprise must take to embrace agility. My extensive research with about two decades of my experience in the IT industry influences the overall strategy, recommendations, and enterprise agility roadmap outlined in the book.

This book will not only provide an in-depth understanding of Enterprise Agility but also introduces a new concept of "_The House of Enterprise Agility_" with its six-strong pillars and describes how the OKR (Objectives and Key Results) model increases Enterprise Agility.

Who Should Read This Book?

This book is specially designed for thought **leaders** who are leading agile transformation efforts, coaching agile or lean frameworks, implementing OKRs, or bringing more business agility to their enterprise. Anyone who is working in an agile or lean environment would benefit from this book, including but not limited to the below roles:

- Corporate Leaders
- SAFe practitioners
- Release Train Engineers
- Scrum Masters
- Project and Product Managers
- Domain experts and Analysts
- Software Engineers
- Test Engineers
- Architects
- UX designers

Why Did I Write This Book?

Though several enterprises have adopted the agile methodology and are continuously following agile principles and practices, none of them are 'truly' agile. Many **enterprises struggle** to keep pace with changing business needs, emerging technologies, and increased competition.

This book is an attempt to reach out to highly talented business and engineering leaders and provide them the steps to increase **Enterprise Agility**. This book will also highlight the need for the OKR model and how it supports the six pillars of EA (Enterprise Agility).

Being a SAFe Process Consultant and a Scrum Coach, I want to bring this fresh perspective of **'true agility'** that has the potential to bring positive results to any enterprise.

How to Read This Book?

If you are new to the concept, I recommend that you read this book from front to back. If you are more interested in the OKR model, you can start with _Chapter 2 - Understanding OKRs._ If you are curious about the six pillars of the _House of Enterprise Agility_, you should start with _Chapter 1 - Enterprise Agility_ and then make your way to the individual chapters dedicated to each of the six pillars.

None of the concepts mentioned in this book are prescriptive and enterprise leaders can choose to adopt what makes sense.

Ready, Set, Go

Set aside a few hours each day to read this book. The chapters that follow provide a step-by-step guide to achieve Enterprise Agility with the OKR model. Happy Reading!

Acknowledgments

First, I would like to express my gratitude to God whose blessings inspired me to write this book. I strongly believe in sharing my knowledge and helping others to succeed.

I would like to acknowledge the support of my parents who have always believed in me. Their unconditional love gives me the courage to move forward.

This book would not have been possible without the support of my loving husband and my genius son. I will take this opportunity to thank them for their continued support and encouragement.

I also thank my colleagues, my friends, and my mentors who trust my abilities and knowledge to write this book.

Chapter 1 –
Enterprise Agility

"Success today requires the agility and drive to constantly rethink, reinvigorate, react, and reinvent."
  - *Bill Gates*

What is Enterprise Agility?

Enterprise Agility is the ability of an enterprise to adapt and change quickly to the ever-changing customer needs, the emergence of new competitors, the development of new technology trends, or a sudden shift in market regulations. The ability of an enterprise to change its direction or pivot to meet its core objectives, increase speed to market, and thrive in a competitive world is called Enterprise Agility. Enterprises with a high degree of business agility can sense both internal and external changes and can respond appropriately

11

to deliver value to their customers without compromising quality.

With Enterprise Agility, an enterprise has an agile way of working across multiple teams, systems, and departments. When the entire organization has an agile mindset, then it has said to have achieved Enterprise Agility. Besides, it is important to scale agile practices across teams and departments for the enterprise to be truly agile.

The three **key drivers** of Enterprise Agility are:

- Flexibility
- Agile Mindset
- Scalability

Flexibility
Traditional managers struggle with the concept of flexibility and quick response to change. They strive to achieve consistent results by following a detailed plan. Thus, they are slow to respond to new market conditions and revised business priorities. On the contrary, agile leaders respond to change faster. They don't expect teams to follow a plan which doesn't provide business value anymore. They encourage their teams to adapt to change and improve continuously.

An agile enterprise revisits its business strategy, enterprise objectives, and product roadmaps regularly. Not only the business plans, but an agile enterprise is also continuously looking to improve its flexibility with funding, talent management, performance reviews, and work allocation. They can mobilize their resources and funds to adapt to their changing environment.

More the flexibility of an enterprise to adapt to its changing environment, the more business agility the enterprise possesses.

Agile Mindset

Most organizations fail in their agile journey due to the lack of an agile mindset across the enterprise. An agile mindset is a key to achieving team agility, building cross-functional teams, enabling technical agility, and developing leadership agility.

Without embracing an agile mindset, teams will not understand the benefits of doing agile or following an agile framework such as Scrum, Extreme Programming, etc. They will continue to iterate and work in their silos. Similarly, without an agile mindset, leaders will continue with their traditional ways to manage teams, holding teams accountable for missing deadlines or not following the initial roadmap.

The organization's culture plays an important role to adopt a growth and learning mindset, operate on agile values and principles, and seek continuous improvement.

Scalability
This is another important driver for Enterprise Agility. An enterprise must scale agility from individual teams to a team of teams or departments and then to the enterprise. Multiple frameworks have evolved with time to scale agile to an enterprise such as Scaled Agile Framework (SAFe), Large-scale Scrum (LeSS), and Disciplined Agile (DA). DevOps practices also emerged as teams started to integrate and deploy their code frequently with increased maturity in technical agility.

To learn about different frameworks that are available to scale agile, read my book, The Basics of Agile and Lean, available on Amazon:

https://www.amazon.com/dp/B07P7T78XZ

Enterprise Agility is achieved when agile processes, values, and principles are embraced at an enterprise level.

Why Enterprise Agility?

In today's fast-growing economy, only enterprises that can adapt quickly to rapidly changing market conditions will survive. Enterprises that are slow to pivot will not be able to keep up with their competitors. Many enterprises have adopted Agile frameworks today and are "doing" agile, however, they have failed to realize its benefits. There are several reasons for this. Some enterprises fail to embrace agile principles and adopt an agile mindset. Others fail to scale agile across teams, portfolios, departments, and the enterprise. Several enterprises still have executives with a traditional mindset who are slow to realign their priorities to rapidly changing business needs.

Teams execute sprints after sprints without understanding how their product priorities align with the enterprise objectives. Thus, even though teams are executing sprints and have a large product backlog, enterprise objectives and goals are not being met.

Often, there is a divide between technology and business teams. Efforts are not aligned with business outcomes. Both technology and business teams strive to prioritize their own needs and are seldom aligned on the highest priority items.

Though teams have adopted the agile methodology and scaled agile methods across the enterprise, they are not measuring what matters most. Even after tracking numerous agility metrics such as predictability scores, velocity charts, burndown charts, etc., enterprises still lag in responding to changing market conditions and achieving enterprise objectives.

In addition to the above, departments such as HR, finance, marketing, sales, legal, compliance, etc. operate in traditional ways. They don't understand the flexibility required to be agile. For example, if an enterprise wants to accelerate one of its objectives that is lagging and needs to reassign its people working on a separate objective to this one, it will need to go through several hoops and internal processes to make this move. There is no simple way to map funding and teams to enterprise objectives.

The House of EA

Let me introduce the **House of EA** to you. This house has 6 key pillars along with a roof and a foundation.

The 6 pillars of the **House of EA** are:

- Planning Agility
- Funding Agility
- Team Agility
- Technical Agility
- Leadership Agility
- HR Agility

The **House of EA** is built on a strong foundation of an agile mindset. Without an agile mindset, none of these pillars can stand. The roof of this house represents the core outcomes of the Enterprise Agility model that are driving business value, responding to change, and built-in quality.

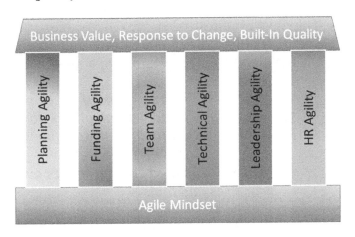

Fig. 1: The House of Enterprise Agility

Agile Mindset: The Foundation

The agile mindset is the foundation to achieve Enterprise Agility. Many enterprises leverage Agile frameworks and practices, however, fail to realize benefits such as increased speed to market, increased productivity, high-quality products, higher employee satisfaction, etc. People's behaviors and attitudes must change to make a difference.

In 2001, 17 visionaries met at Snowbird ski resort in the Wasatch mountains of Utah to find common ground among different approaches to software development. The outcome was <u>a Manifesto for Agile Software Development</u> that was signed by all participants.

The Agile Manifesto provides core values and principles that are fundamental to embracing the agile mindset. The Manifesto states:

"We are uncovering better ways of developing software by doing it and helping others do it. Through this work we have come to value:

- ***Individuals and interactions*** *over processes and tools*

- ***Working software*** *over comprehensive documentation*

- ***Customer collaboration*** *over contract negotiation*

- ***Responding to change*** *over following a plan*

That is, while there is value in the items on the right, we value the items on the left more."

Besides these values, the Agile Manifesto also consists of 12 principles as below:

- Our highest priority is to satisfy the customer through early and continuous delivery of valuable software.

- Welcome changing requirements, even late in development. Agile processes harness change for the customer's competitive advantage.

- Deliver working software frequently, from a couple of weeks to a couple of months, with a preference to the shorter timescale.

- Business people and developers must work together daily throughout the project.

- Build projects around motivated individuals. Give them the environment and support they need and trust them to get the job done.

- The most efficient and effective method of conveying information to and within a development team is a face-to-face conversation.

- Working software is the primary measure of progress.

- Agile processes promote sustainable development. The sponsors, developers, and users should be able to maintain a constant pace indefinitely.

- Continuous attention to technical excellence and good design enhances agility.

- Simplicity--the art of maximizing the amount of work not done--is essential.

- The best architectures, requirements, and designs emerge from self-organizing teams.

- At regular intervals, the team reflects on how to become more effective, then tunes and adjusts its behavior accordingly.

Grand principles that generate no action are a mere vapor. Conversely, specific practices in the absence of guiding principles are often inappropriately used.
- Jim Highsmith, Author

Read my blog "What are the 12 Agile Principles?' on Medium:

https://medium.com/@authoraditiagarwal/what-are-the-agile-principles-3e4d3ae0b227

Business value, response to change, and built-in quality: The roof

The roof of the EA house comprises of business value, response to change, and built-in quality. These are the core outcomes of achieving Enterprise Agility. Let's dive into each of them.

1. Business value: The roof

This is one of the core outcomes of Enterprise Agility. With Enterprise Agility, enterprises can easily pivot to meet their enterprise objectives, **deliver business value**, and thrive in a competitive world.

2. Response to change: The roof

Agile enterprises can quickly respond to changing market conditions, emerging technology trends, or competitor threats. With Enterprise Agility, teams or departments across an enterprise adopt an agile mindset **to embrace change** and deliver business value.

In recent years, technologies such as Artificial Intelligence, Machine Learning, Blockchain, Cryptocurrencies, etc. have seen exponential growth. Enterprises that are agile can quickly adapt to these new technologies, whereas other organizations with traditional mindsets or limited agility will take much longer to respond.

3. Built-in quality: The roof

Built-in quality ensures that products that are delivered meet high-quality standards throughout the development cycle.

"Inspection does not improve the quality, nor guarantee quality. Inspection is too late. The quality, good or bad, is already in the product. Quality cannot be inspected into a

product or service; it must be built into it."

- W. Edwards Deming

With Enterprise Agility, comes Technical Agility which covers quality aspects such as **design quality, code quality**, and **deployment quality**.

During product development, design options are kept flexible for as long as possible, instead of having an upfront design. This promotes flexibility in the design process, enables the team to experiment with the available options, and allows them to choose the best design approach. The high-quality design also considers factors such as cost of development, maintainability, scalability, performance, etc.

The higher the code quality, the more the speed to market. Technical Agility encourages collaboration, transparency, and ownership so that everyone can maintain a high-quality code. Practices such as writing unit tests, pair programming, and test-driven development encourage engineers to maintain code quality.

The ability to integrate and deploy code frequently via a continuous delivery pipeline indicates the DevOps maturity and the deployment quality of an enterprise.

"Be a yardstick of quality. Some people aren't used to an environment where excellence is expected."
- Steve Jobs

The 6 Pillars of the EA House

- Planning Agility
- Funding Agility
- Team Agility
- Technical Agility
- Leadership Agility
- HR Agility

1. Planning Agility

Planning Agility represents the flexibility of an enterprise to change a product's roadmap and its priorities considering changing market conditions or emerging technology trends.

2. Funding Agility

Funding Agility is closely related to Planning Agility. To quickly adapt to changing market conditions or emerging technologies, an enterprise must have the flexibility to move its funds around, across teams, departments, and products, depending on the need.

3. Team Agility

Enterprise Agility can only be achieved when all teams across an enterprise have adopted the agile mindset, values, and principles. For a team to be agile, they must adapt to change, learn to collaborate, self-organize their work, and consistently deliver high-quality work to generate business value.

4. Technical Agility

Teams achieve technical agility by leveraging engineering practices to deliver high-quality products quickly. Some of these practices include a continuous focus on architecture and quality design, test-driven development (TDD), behavior-driven development (BDD), continuous integration (CI), continuous deployment (CD), creating unit tests, and ensuring code quality.

5. Leadership Agility

This is an important competency for enterprise executives and leaders to develop. Leadership Agility is the ability to make effective decisions, inspire people, and initiate action with an understanding of what it takes to lead in a rapidly changing world. With more agility, leaders become more collaborative and proactive in leading teams and driving organizational changes.

6. HR Agility

In an agile enterprise, it is important to integrate HR and other supporting departments such as Finance, Sales, Marketing, etc. with the product development process and introduce agility into their work.

Summary

Enterprise Agility is the ability for enterprises to embrace the agile mindset, adapt quickly to the rapidly changing circumstances, and deliver high-quality products or services that deliver business value. The foundation of the house of Enterprise Agility is the agile mindset. The business value, the response to change, and the built-in quality represent the roof of the house. There are 6 key pillars of the Enterprise Agility House which will be covered in the remaining chapters of this book as listed below:

- Planning Agility
- Funding Agility
- Team Agility

- Technical Agility
- Leadership Agility
- HR Agility

Exercise 1: Test your knowledge

- What is Enterprise Agility (EA)?

- What is the House of EA?

Exercise 2: Brainstorming

- Meet with your team and brainstorm practical examples to adopt the agile mindset and principles at work.

- Brainstorm ideas that can increase the business agility of your enterprise.

Exercise 3: Develop the mindset

- View *the Agile Maturity Assessment activity worksheet* (see link below) and assess agile maturity for your enterprise, portfolio, or team. Access the worksheet on Google Docs:

*https://docs.google.com/document/d/1
DU7J5geirfrNgEHgbsjciAckGyobB3beQ
XzclJzuwzY/edit?usp=sharing*

*You may use the space below to jot down your
thoughts on the exercises above.*

Chapter 2 – Understanding OKRs

"By clearing the line of sight to everyone's objectives, OKRs expose redundant efforts and save time and money."
- *John Doerr, Measure What Matters*

What are OKRs?

OKR stands for **Objectives and Key Results**. It is a simple management methodology and an agile goal-setting system that enables everyone to align with enterprise objectives and to visualize the progress made towards them.

Founded by Intel CEO, **Andy Grove**, in the 1970s, the OKRs methodology was first adopted by Google in 1999. Since then, OKRs have helped **Google** and several other enterprises to stay focused, create transparency, gain alignment, and achieve better results. Today, several organizations across all sectors such as Spotify, LinkedIn, Walmart, Bill and Melinda Gates Foundation, and others are using this framework to set and achieve audacious goals.

In 1999, **John Doerr**, a venture capitalist, introduced OKRs to Google. In his meeting with **Larry Page** and **Sergey Brin**, co-founders of Google, he introduced the OKR system and explained how it can help Google to achieve its aggressive growth targets. In his book, ***Measure What Matters***, John revealed how the system of OKRs has helped organizations achieve agility and explosive growth.

John Doerr's formula for OKRs is:
I will (Objective) as measured by (set of Key Results).

Objectives define 'what' is to be achieved. They are qualitative, significant, concrete, short, inspirational, memorable, and ambitious. Each objective could have 2-5 key results. Enterprise objectives provide a purpose for the entire enterprise. Similarly, a portfolio or a department objective unites the entire portfolio or the department to achieve the same.

Key Results define 'how' we achieve the objectives. They are a set of measurable milestones for each objective to track progress towards achieving the objective. They are quantitative, specific, measurable, time-bound, verifiable, and aggressive, but realistic. When key results are complete, the objective is necessarily achieved. If the objective is not achieved even after completing the key results, it implies that the key results were not written correctly for the objective.

OKRs are frequently set, tracked, and evaluated, usually every quarter. OKRs are agile. They provide a framework for an enterprise to achieve its goals via the definition of measurable and time-bound actions, alignment across the enterprise, and tracking progress against them.

Why OKRs?

OKRs bring several benefits to an enterprise, portfolio or department, or team. Some of those benefits are listed as follows:

Focus and Prioritization
Often, product and engineering teams have conflicting thoughts on product priorities. Such a conflict makes it difficult for the product team

to align on the product roadmap, which in turn, impacts the team's morale and productivity.

OKRs provide a framework to both product and engineering leaders to visualize the product strategy, create and map the product objectives to the enterprise objectives, define specific and measurable KRs, and align on the product roadmap. OKRs impel leaders to make hard choices.

"OKRs are clear vessels for leaders' priorities and insights."
- John Doerr

Transparency and Alignment
The OKRs framework acts as a communication tool for leaders, product teams, engineering teams, dependent teams, and individual contributors. OKRs are openly shared with everyone in the enterprise.

The mapping between enterprise OKRs to a department or group's OKRs, then to a product or a team OKRs, and finally to an individual's OKRs is open and transparent. This fosters better coordination and alignment with dependent products and teams within the enterprise.

"You need to overcome the tug of people against you as you reach for high goals."
- George S, Patton

Measurement and Tracking

OKRs are driven by the measurement of key results. Key Results (KRs) are measured and tracked periodically. If a KR is at risk, then actions are taken to mitigate the risk or revise the KR if needed.

"If the focus is delivering something the customer wants, you must move from primarily measuring outputs to primarily measuring outcomes."
- Mario E. Moreira

Motivation and Excellence

People are thirsty for purpose, to understand why it matters what they are doing. OKRs provide a framework to map the team's objectives to the corporate ones.

Stretch or aspirational OKRs motivate the team to excel by going above and beyond their commitments. Since teams have room to fail with aspirational OKRs, they work freely, bring out their creativities, collaborate better, stay accountable, and experiment harder.

"Do something that scares you every day."
        - Eleanor Roosevelt

Enhanced Agility
With the frequent measurement of KRs and reassessment of objectives, the enterprise stays agile with its business strategy and outcomes. Such an enterprise is well-equipped and prepared to respond quickly to changing market conditions or emerging technology trends.

"Agility is the ability to adapt and respond to change. Agile organizations view change as an opportunity, not a threat."
        - Jim Highsmith

Decision Making
OKRs enable data-driven, informed, and proactive decision-making. If any of the key results being tracked is underperforming,

appropriate decisions can be taken at the right time to modify or abandon an objective and reallocate resources elsewhere, as needed.

"We must realize—and act on the realization—that if we try to focus on everything, we focus on nothing."
- John Doerr

Types of OKRs

There are different types of OKRs. Let's understand what they mean in this section so you can decide which ones to write for your team, portfolio, or enterprise.

Strategic vs tactical OKRs

Strategic OKRs are long-term annual OKRs set for the enterprise. These represent the strategic themes or core focus areas for the enterprise. **Tactical OKRs,** on the contrary, are short-term quarterly OKRs that are set for a department, a product, or a team. These represent specific OKRs that support strategic OKRs.

Let's understand the difference between the two with a *practical example*.

<u>Example: Strategic OKRs</u>
One of the strategic objectives of a fictional retail store is:

"Increase revenue by 20%"

Example KRs for this objective are:

- *Open 2 new stores by Q2 this year*
- *Increase online sales by 30% by Q3*

<u>Example: Tactical OKRs</u>
One of the tactical objectives for the above retail store example is:

"Increase QoQ unique# of online visitors"

Example KRs for this objective are:

- *Increase system availability to 99% by Q1*
- *Increase search engine rankings for targeted keywords by 30% by Q2 this year*

Committed vs aspirational OKRs
Committed OKRs are predictable OKRs that teams target to achieve 100%. Aspirational OKRs are non-predictable, high-risk items that teams try to achieve 40-70% (varies by organization).

Let's understand the difference between the two with a practical example.

Example: Committed OKRs
For our fictional retail store, a sample committed objective may be:

"Provide the best-in-class online shopping experience"

Example KRs for this objective are:

- *Delight online customers with enhanced catalog and search features by Q2*
- *Improve online traffic by 20% by Q3*

Example: Aspirational OKRs
A sample aspirational objective for the retail store could be:

"Allow customers to compare prices with other competitive retail stores"

Example KRs for this aspirational objective could be:

- *Reduce abandoned shopping carts by 30% by the end of Q3*
- *Increase return customers by 20% this year*

Value-driven vs milestone-based OKRs
Value-driven OKRs represent outcomes and business value delivered to the customers, whereas, milestone-based OKRs focus on activities such as analysis, research, development, delivery, and so on.

Examples for value-driven KRs

- *Increase net promoter score by 20%*
- *Increase organic traffic to the site by 30%*
- *Increase employee retention by 40%*

Examples for milestone-based KRs

- *Complete technical feasibility by Feb*
- *Build the proof-of-concept by March*
- *Launch MVP to selected customers by Apr*
- *Iterate and roll out to all customers by July*

How to write good OKRs?

Let's look at the criteria for writing good OKRs along with a few *practical examples*.

Criteria for writing good Objectives
- Does the objective align with the enterprise's strategy?
- Is the objective ambitious?
- Does the objective inspire others?

- Is the objective time-bound?
- Is the objective value-driven instead of milestone-driven?

Examples of well-written objectives

- Increase the brand value of the enterprise by the end of this year
- Increase SEO rankings of the website content by the end of the 3rd quarter
- Acquire new customers by month-end
- Increase organic traffic on the company's website by month-end
- Provide leadership training to all colleagues by the end of this year
- Eradicate hunger from the world by the end of 2025.
- Create consistent user experiences by the end of the second quarter
- Reward and delight loyal customers by the end of this year
- Provide best customer service across all physical and online stores by year-end
- Be agile across the enterprise by the end of the year

Examples of poorly-written objectives

- Increase revenue (not time-bound)
- Maintain existing product suite (not inspiring or ambitious)

- Redesign website by year-end (milestone-driven rather than value-driven)
- Ongoing platform support (not ambitious, not inspiring, not time-bound)

Criteria for writing good Key Results
- Is the KR time-bound?
- Is the KR measurable?
- Is the KR specific and achievable?
- Is the KR metric-driven instead of milestone-driven?

Examples of well-written key results
- Increase revenue by $100K by the end of this quarter
- Publish 5 new brand videos ads on YouTube by the end of this month
- Acquire 50% new online customers by the end of this year
- Increase unique online visitors by 30% on the company's website by month-end
- Conduct 8-10 leadership training workshops every month
- Provide 50% more food to hungry kids in Somalia by the end of this quarter
- Increase adoption of the reusable react component 'A' by 30%

- Increase reward points redemption options by 20% this month
- Reduce customer complaints by 80% before the end of the second quarter
- Coach 5-7 large teams or about 500 new people on agile principles by the end of this quarter

Examples of poorly-written key results
- Publish new content on the website (not time-bound, not measurable)
- Conduct leadership training this month (not measurable)
- Increase sales this month (not metric-driven, not measurable, not specific)
- Provide best customer service (no specific, not time-bound, not measurable)
- Increase adoption of the software by month-end (not measurable)
- Test the new software product by the end of this month (milestone-driven; not metric-driven)

Common OKR mistakes

The below section covers some common mistakes made when implementing OKRs in an enterprise. Knowing these mistakes will help you to make informed decisions for your enterprise, portfolio, or team.

Setting too many objectives and KRs
Often, teams set too many OKRs for themselves such that it becomes a high, overwhelming list of to-do items. It is important to prioritize and define only 3-5 top-priority outcomes.

Defining non-measurable KRs
Another common mistake when introducing OKRs to an enterprise is the definition of non-measurable key results. It is important to write KRs such that they are specific, time-bound, and measurable to realize benefits.

Setting milestone or task-based KRs
A very common mistake that most teams make is setting milestone-based OKRs instead of value-based OKRs. Such objectives are geared towards initiatives or projects and seldom help in measuring outcomes or progress made towards achieving enterprise goals.

Not tracking against OKRs
Teams that set OKRs but are not serious to track them regularly fail to realize OKR benefits. It is important to track the completion of KRs at regular intervals and assess if they are still achievable. If these become unachievable or irrelevant, they should be revised or dropped

altogether. Without reviewing, measuring, and tracking OKRs, there's an increased risk of wasting time and effort towards achieving an undesired or unattainable objective.

Creating team OKRs in silos

OKRs should be created in collaboration with other teams. Often, teams work in their silos and define team-specific OKRs. OKRs' benefits are best realized when team OKRs map to enterprise OKRs and when a team defined their OKRs in collaboration with other dependent teams.

Defining OKRs that are too easy

This is another trap that many teams fall into. They tend to define easily achievable OKRs such that they appear more productive and efficient as compared to other teams in the enterprise. However, the fact is that such behavior fails to inspire people and achieve complete benefits. Objectives should be written such that they are ambitious and inspiring to motivate others.

Implementing the OKR model in small pockets within an enterprise

The toughest part to implement a new model within an enterprise is to seek alignment from all the different leaders and individuals across portfolios or teams. Often, change agents try to implement the OKR model with a handful of teams. This implementation approach does not scale as the OKR model won't work if only a portion of individuals and leaders are committed. It is important to seek buy-in from all people in the enterprise for this model to work effectively.

Creating rigid processes around OKRs

Another common mistake is the creation of rigid processes and tight control around OKRs. For this model to thrive, it is best to stay agile with the practices involved in defining or tracking OKRs. Teams should not only have visibility into enterprise OKRs, but they should also have the flexibility to define local or team-specific OKRs. Teams should also have the flexibility to modify or abandon an OKR that is not feasible or achievable.

Expecting quick and perfect results

Often, an enterprise expects a quick turnaround and visible results upon implementing the OKR model. Leaders fail to understand that it takes time to fully adopt this model and achieve their defined OKRs. Patience is important as people learn and adopt this model.

Moreover, it may not work perfectly the first time it is implemented. An enterprise may define too easy or too ambitious OKRs to start with. If an enterprise achieves 100% of its

OKRs, they have too easy OKRs and should set more ambitious ones. If an enterprise achieves 60-70% of its OKRs, then it is doing something right.

When not to use OKRs

OKRs are not suitable for all enterprises. The below section lists a few scenarios when OKRs are not the best choice for an organization.

When OKRs are not agile: When OKRs are rigid, the model does not provide any room for people to make mistakes, abandon OKRs, or be agile. The OKR model is meant to inspire people and drive better alignment, focus, engagement, and performance. For example, if an OKR was abandoned in the middle of the quarter, people working on that specific OKR should not be penalized during their annual performance reviews. Instead, they should be appropriately rewarded for their sincere efforts to drive goals forward and their courage to bring out risks associated with the aligned OKR.

When OKRs don't flow quickly down the corporate hierarchy: Some enterprises find it difficult to align corporate OKRs with portfolio and team OKRs. Thus, it takes a considerable amount of time for them to cascade strategic OKRs to the teams. For a quarterly OKR, if it takes about a month to map the same across different portfolios and teams, then teams will not have enough time to work towards it. This delay introduces a high probability of not achieving strategic OKRs.

When conflicting priorities are tough to resolve: With conflicting priorities, planning becomes a nightmare and it might consume a considerable amount of time and effort to lock down OKRs for each quarter. This is more relevant to team-specific or tactical OKRs. In such scenarios, when team leaders struggle to align on common objectives, teams might not start working towards the OKRs until the end of the quarter. This decreases team morale due to the lack of substantial progress on team OKRs.

When there is not enough time or focus to create well-written OKRs: When teams don't have enough time or motivation to create well-written OKRs, they end up with poorly-written ones that lead to dissatisfaction and poor results. Such teams fail to realize OKR benefits and soon abandon the model.

Implementing OKRs

Now that you understand OKRs, you are ready to dive into the implementation of the same. It's very important to implement OKRs the right way and plan for OKR training needs for your team or enterprise.

There are two approaches to implementing OKRs. You should understand the pros and cons of each and then decide which one is the best for your enterprise and team.

- Pilot / Partial approach
- Full approach

Pilot / partial rollout approach
In this approach, OKRs are first rolled out to only one portfolio, department, or team. Some organizations prefer a partial rollout to only people leaders. With the partial approach, the OKR model is piloted to a subset of people of the enterprise. The pilot group may be a specific team, a specific portfolio or department, a specific business unit, a solution train, an agile release train, or a specific group of leaders.

The core **benefits** of the pilot/partial rollout approach are listed below:

- Containment of risk or uncertainty to a subset of people or business functions
- Minimum disruption of business
- Early feedback on the adoption process

The **drawbacks** of this approach are:

- Slow adoption as it will take longer for everyone to get onboard.
- The real benefits of OKRs will not be realized until the model is rolled out to everyone in the enterprise.

Full rollout approach

In this approach, OKRs are rolled out to the entire organization all at once. With full-rollout, some organizations prefer a **top-down** approach, where corporate OKRs are defined first. The corporate OKRs, then, are mapped to the OKRs of either a business unit, a department, or a program. Those OKRs are then mapped to the team and individual-level OKRs. In a **bottom-up** approach, individual and team OKRs are defined first, which are then rolled up to a business unit, a department, or a program level. The program-level OKRs are then further rolled up to corporate OKRs. Most organizations who adopt the OKR model prefer a combination of both top-down and bottom-up approaches such that teams can align their objectives with corporate objectives and can also define team-specific or tactical OKRs, as needed. Irrespective of a top-down or a bottom-up approach, the full rollout to the enterprise is the fastest way to embrace OKRs.

The **benefits** of the full rollout approach are:

- Leaders' buy-in and commitment
- Faster adoption across the enterprise
- Early realization of OKR benefits

The **drawbacks** of this approach are:

- Higher risk of disrupting product roadmaps or services.
- Extensive planning and tracking required for smooth deployment
- Upfront budget required for enterprise-wide OKR training/product.

Common OKR products or software providers

There are a variety of OKR providers that exist in the market today. In this section, I will highlight a few popular ones out there. This section is not my endorsement of any of these products or providers.

Weekdone
This is a popular OKR tool to align enterprise, department, team, and personal goals, share and track progress, view real-time team's dashboard, track team activities, enable simple online check-ins, view trend reports, hold

private employee reviews and discussions, and much more. Weekdone enables everyone to work towards the strategic enterprise vision.

Weekdone supports dashboard and reports in Atlassian's JIRA, Asana, and Basecamp. Besides these, Weekdone can also be integrated with Google, Slack, and Zapier.

This product is FREE forever for 1-3 users. For more users, pricing is available on their site. They have extensive resources available in the form of FREE eBooks, reporting templates, newsletters, blogs, and much more.

Weekdone: https://weekdone.com/

Atlassian's JIRA: https://www.atlassian.com/software/jira

Asana: https://asana.com/

Basecamp: https://basecamp.com/

Slack: https://slack.com/

Zapier: https://zapier.com/

Weekdone pricing: https://weekdone.com/prices

*Free eBooks on Weekdone:
https://weekdone.com/ebook/okr-goal-setting-guide-template*

Perdoo
This is an OKR software that enables leaders and teams to focus on work that matters the most, align departments and teams, track organizational priorities, measure outcomes, achieve remarkable results, and more.

Perdoo is a paid product and its pricing is available on its website. You can also request a demo and access their resources to view helpful videos or download free eBooks. It also supports integration with Google and Slack.

Perdoo: https://www.perdoo.com/

Pricing: https://www.perdoo.com/pricing/

Atiim
Attim is another goal management tool to set and track OKRs, monitor progress, align with everyone, support individual OKRs, and measure what matters. This software integrates with Google SSO, Slack, Okta, JIRA, and Salesforce.

It is a paid product with pricing options available on its website. The site also hosts several useful resources such as the OKR library, blog, templates, examples, and webinars.

Atiim: https://www.atiim.com/

Pricing: https://www.atiim.com/pricing/

7Geese

Another OKR software is 7Geese that supports OKRs, continuous feedback, employee recognition, private conversations, career management, and more. It provides integration with Human Resource Information System (HRIS) software, Slack, Gmail, and Asana.

It is a paid product with different plans. Pricing and plans can be viewed on their website.

7Geese: https://7geese.com/

Pricing: https://7geese.com/pricing/

15Five

This is another popular software that supports OKRs, goal management, 360-degree feedback, employee engagement, development plans, performance tracking, and more.

15Five is a paid product with different pricing plans for its customers. It has rich resources including eBooks, webinars, videos, and podcasts. It also provides integration with Google SSO, Slack, and HRIS software - BambooHR & Namely.

15Five: https://www.15five.com/

Summary

OKR stands for objectives and key results. They promote prioritization, alignment, transparency, a common purpose, motivation, and enterprise agility. There are different types of OKRs as summarized below:

- Strategic
- Tactical
- Committed
- Aspirational
- Value-driven
- Milestone-driven

Teams should follow the core criteria, as described in this chapter, to write good OKRs. Enterprises should avoid the common OKR mistakes described. The OKR model may not work for all enterprises.

Exercise 1: Test your knowledge

- What are OKRs?

- What are the different types of OKRs?
- How will you implement the OKR model in your organization? Write down 3 steps required to get started.

Exercise 2: Define OKRs for your team with a top-down approach

- Write your corporate and portfolio OKRs.

- Brainstorm with your team and map top-level corporate objectives to your team. Define team objectives.

- Select the top 2 objectives for your team.

- Brainstorm and write 2-5 KRs for each team objective.

- Discuss how these OKRs should be tracked.

Exercise 3: Define OKRs with a bottom-up approach

- Brainstorm and write objectives for a team.

- Extend this exercise to other teams in your portfolio, group, or department.

- Roll up team objectives into program, portfolio, or department-level objectives.

- Select the top 3 objectives and define 2-5 KRs for each of these.

You may use the space below to jot down your thoughts on the exercises above.

Chapter 3 – Planning Agility

"The greatest danger in times of turbulence is not the turbulence - it is to act with yesterday's logic."
- Peter Drucker

What is Planning Agility?

Planning Agility is the ability to change plans regularly and quickly. The world is moving fast, and our surrounding conditions are continuously changing. Factors such as extreme weather, political instability, social media, press releases, customer intent, increased competition, new technology trends, stock market fluctuations, etc. demand plans to be agile such that enterprises can adapt and respond quickly to such changes. No matter how perfect a plan looks at any given point in time, it will require a change in the future.

"The rate of change is not going to slow down anytime soon. If anything, competition in most industries will probably speed up even more in the next few decades."
- John P. Kotter

With the traditional plan-driven "Waterfall" approach, there is limited flexibility to change the project plan. In this approach, any change to a project plan requires a formal change control request that triggers an impact assessment to the baselined scope, budget, or schedule. This rigid process slows down plan changes.

In the early 2000s, the pace, scale, and breadth of technology changes grew many folds that changed the way companies used to operate. Several enterprises became aware of the inherent bottlenecks with the traditional plan-driven approach and adopted the agile methodology for software development.

Today, though enterprises are "**doing**" agile, they still have a traditional mindset when it comes to defining their business strategy and priorities. Leaders spend a lot of their time and energy during year-end planning meetings to align on business priorities for the following year. This upfront planning for the year, though important, is not enough.

Enterprises that claim to be "agile" still rely on budget and timeline forecasts when funding projects or initiatives. This traditional budgeting and planning require decisions to be made **'too early'** with several assumptions. Once an initiative is underway, the needs of the business change and it becomes difficult for the enterprise to then re-allocate budget and resources to a different initiative at short notice.

For an enterprise to be "**truly agile**", planning should be frequent, and plans should be flexible. Instead of a one-time exhaustive planning exercise, agile enterprises need quarterly planning meetings where leaders revisit their priorities and align on short-term plans for the upcoming quarter. Frequent discussions enable Planning Agility for the enterprise and allow the realignment of priorities, plans, budgets, and resources to meet changing business or technology needs.

"In preparing for battle I have always found that plans are useless, but planning is indispensable."
- Dwight D. Eisenhower

The **planning frequency** should be carefully chosen and aligned within the enterprise. If the frequency is too high, then the risk of not delivering any business value becomes too high. In this state where business priorities are changing every month or every other week, the team gets disoriented and confused with ever-changing priorities and fails to deliver value. On the contrary, if the frequency is too low, then the risk of falling behind the competition increases. In this state, enterprises fail to react quickly to changing business needs and emerging technology trends. Though teams work hard to achieve business goals, the value delivered is never enough.

"Speed is everything. It is the indispensable ingredient to competitiveness."
- Jack Welch

Many enterprises choose to revisit their priorities and goals every quarter instead of a one-time annual planning exercise. This gives them enough opportunity to stay ahead of their competition and reprioritize their goals to match with emerging technology trends or the latest market conditions while leaving enough room for teams to focus on quarterly objectives and deliver something meaningful.

SAFe and Planning Agility

Does SAFe (Scaled Agile Framework) promote Planning Agility? With SAFe, the prioritized product features are reviewed and aligned at the start of every PI (Program Increment), which is typically 8-12 weeks long. Teams analyze the upcoming prioritized features and user stories and then summarize the information in a business language to form team PI objectives. Team objectives are then rolled up to the *Program Level* which are further rolled up to the *Large Solution Level* objectives. This is the **bottom-up approach** to build objectives for the enterprise. The **drawback** with this approach is that the rolled-up objectives at the corporate level **may not align** with the strategic vision of the enterprise.

Moreover, if an enterprise needs to adapt to the changing market conditions or emerging technology or respond to a recent threat by its competitors, its corporate strategy and objectives will need to be revised and this change needs to quickly flow down the hierarchy at a product level. With a bottom-up approach, adapting to a change is a **slow**

process with each product team realigning its priorities and features for the upcoming PI.

OKRs and Planning Agility

The OKR model (covered in Chapter 2) is a combination of both **top-down and bottom-up approaches** that encourages the quarterly definition of enterprise and product priorities.

This iterative planning with continued focus enables an enterprise to "be agile" and adapt quickly to changes. With OKRs, enterprises can define quarterly objectives that inspire people and provide them with a greater purpose. At the end of every quarter, teams measure their KRs for the current quarter and define their OKRs for the next quarter. This framework provides the flexibility to **reprioritize** and **realign** objectives and priorities every quarter.

Even during a quarter, if a team realizes that an earlier defined OKR is unachievable, the specific objective gets abandoned. Similarly, mid-quarter or during an OKR cycle, if a new objective gets defined at a corporate level, the programs and teams quickly adjust their objectives to align with the corporate objectives. OKRs are flexible and they change with the business or environment changes, as needed.

With the OKR model, both **strategic and tactical priorities** are continuously updated at regular intervals. Such an enterprise, using the OKR model, is said to have **Planning Agility**.

Enterprise Roadmap

An enterprise must have clarity on its core objectives and goals that support and strengthen its vision. A roadmap is a high-level plan that describes how and when the objectives are likely to be achieved.

"Doing the right thing is more important than doing the thing right."
- Peter Drucker

The OKR-driven or a goal-oriented roadmap is much more effective than a feature-driven roadmap as the OKR-driven roadmap reflects the shared vision, objectives, and goals for the enterprise. The goal-oriented roadmap also reduces conflicts over competing priorities or features due to its targeted focus on OKRs. This type of roadmap also aligns with the agile methodology as agile teams only commit work for the upcoming iteration.

The OKR-driven, quarterly roadmap for an enterprise should include the below items at a minimum:

- Prioritized <u>strategic objectives</u> for a quarter that provide a sense of purpose and inspiration to the enterprise
- Prioritized <u>measurable results</u>
- Associated <u>metrics</u> for each objective
- Specific themes, initiatives, or capabilities that map to the aligned OKRs

Product Roadmap

Every product, too, must have a product strategy and a **product roadmap** to help realize the product vision and its objectives. The OKR-driven product roadmap must have quarterly **product objectives** that map to the quarterly strategic or corporate objectives. The product roadmap may also include release information, milestones, status indicators, major themes, Epics, and features.

The product roadmap is a powerful tool to have a continued focus on the purpose, create alignment with product stakeholders, measure progress, and adjust the plan as needed.

Roadmap Templates

Let's look at a few common roadmap templates with OKRs as below. You can also view these templates on Google Docs.

https://docs.google.com/presentation/d/1_gkn cew7wMkZkVtzz8n2ZM_IFVQVcG2RBUKwJk3 nU5M/edit?usp=sharing

Template #1:

	Jan - Mar	Apr - Jun	July - Sep	Oct - Dec
Objectives				
Key Results				
Features				
Metrics				

Fig. 2: Product Roadmap Template #1

This simple roadmap template covers the product objectives and key results for each quarter. The template also captures product features necessary to achieve quarterly objectives and metrics required to track completion.

Enterprises that measure and track OKRs every month or at every PI (product increment) boundary will need to customize the above template to reflect the desired duration.

Template #2:

	Jan - Mar	Apr - Jun	July - Sep	Oct - Dec
Objectives				
Key Results				
Themes/ Capabilities/ EPICs				
Product Features				
Metrics				

Fig. 3: Product Roadmap Template #2

The above template captures quarterly OKRs for the product along with product features and metrics associated with each objective. The template also displays the high-level categories/buckets that the features are rolled into. Some organizations prefer to roll up product features into EPICs for reporting purposes, while other organizations may want to track the mapping of product objectives with enterprise themes or program capabilities.

Again, enterprises that measure and track OKRs every month or at every PI (product increment) boundary will need to customize the above template to reflect the desired duration.

Template #3:

Product Name, Vision, and Strategy				
	Jan - Mar	Apr - Jun	July - Sep	Oct - Dec
Milestones / Release Dates				
Enterprise OKRs				
Objectives				
Key Results				
Features				
Metrics				

Fig. 4: Product Roadmap Template #3

There are two additional rows in the above template - one to capture the release dates or major milestones and the other is to highlight enterprise OKRs such that the mapping between enterprise OKRs and product OKRs is explicit on the roadmap.

Based on your specific needs, you can leverage the most suitable product roadmap template from above or customize these and create your own, as needed.

Sample Roadmaps

Today, agile enterprises focus on setting objectives, defining priorities, and creating roadmaps only for the products and services that they offer. For an enterprise to be "truly agile", **internal departments** such as marketing, sales, training, legal, compliance, HR, etc. should also have Planning Agility. They should also set their objectives, track progress, measure key results, and create quarterly roadmaps to best serve the interests of the enterprise. In the below section, let's look at a few **sample** roadmaps for internal groups or departments of an enterprise.

Sample Marketing Roadmap

	Jan - Mar	Apr - Jun	July - Sep	Oct - Dec
Objectives	Know your customer	Generate new leads	Increase customer outreach	Increase speed to market
Key Results	Conduct at least 3 user testing sessions per month Publish market research and primary personas by the end of March	Launch at least 3 new campaigns every month Grow new customers by at least 5% every week	Publish a newsletter every month Publish at least 3 articles on the site every week	Run at least 5 new campaigns with the automated platform every month
Features	Conduct market research Conduct user testing sessions Create user personas	Launch social media campaigns Launch print media campaigns Perform keyword research Optimize SEO tags Improve site performance	Publish newsletters Publish reference articles and how-to guides	Deploy and adopt an automated marketing platform
Metrics	% of users participated during market research # of user testing sessions per month	# of social and print media campaigns launched per month # of unique site visitors Click through rate	# of newsletters published # of articles published	# of campaigns launched on the automated platform

Fig. 5: Sample Marketing Roadmap

Sample HR Roadmap

	Jan - Mar	Apr - Jun	July - Sep	Oct - Dec
Objectives	Hire the best talent in the industry	Increase employee engagement	Enable career growth of all employees	Improve incentives
Key Results	Increase hiring by 5% this quarter	Improve employee survey scores by 30%	Increase mentoring and training opportunities for all employees by 20%	100% adoption of the new incentive program across the enterprise
Features	Create a recruitment panel for niche technologies Schedule recruitment drives in colleges Conduct interviews Generate offer letters	Manage team building events and activities Conduct employee surveys	Arrange niche trainings for employees Rollout a mentor-mentee program	Create team incentives Rollout the new incentive program
Metrics	# of new hires per month	# of team building events per month Employee survey scores	# of employees who attended niche trainings Average % of new competencies achieved % increase in new promotions this quarter	# of teams who adopted the new incentive program

Fig. 6: Sample HR Roadmap

You can also view these sample roadmaps on *Google Docs*:

> https://docs.google.com/presentation/d/12vZ5
> z4uJWhGML2MQC2Yf8HETtMq8PyEVP5VxtV
> --4AU/edit?usp=sharing

Summary

Planning Agility is the ability to change plans quickly. For an enterprise to be "**truly agile**", planning should be frequent, and plans should be flexible. We also covered roadmap templates and a few sample roadmaps with this chapter. Those slides are also available on Google Docs for your reference.

Exercise 1: Test your knowledge

- What is Planning Agility?

- How does the OKR model promote Planning Agility?

- Which of these two frameworks is better to promote Planning Agility - SAFe or OKRs? and Why?

Exercise 2: Create a roadmap

- Finalize your roadmap template

- Know your enterprise OKRs

- Define product objectives and key results for each quarter or each PI

- Map the features that will achieve the desired objectives for each quarter
- Define specific metrics to track each product objective

- Complete the template with any additional details needed such as release name, release date, themes, EPICs, capabilities, etc.

- Align the roadmap with the product stakeholders

You may use the space below to jot down your thoughts on the exercises above.

Enterprise Agility with OKRs

Chapter 4 – Funding Agility

"The game of business used to be like football: size mattered. Then it changed to basketball: speed and agility. Today, business is more like chess. Customer priorities change continually, and the signals given by these changes are vital clues to the next cycle of growth."
-   Adrian Slywotzky

What is Funding Agility?

Funding Agility for an enterprise means an ability for an enterprise to move funds quickly from one department or team to another. With Planning Agility, enterprises also need the flexibility to move funds around. For example, if a department or a team abandons an unachievable objective whereas another department or team needs additional funding to work on a stretch objective, the enterprise should be able to move funds between the two departments or teams easily without any issues.

What failed?

With the traditional plan-driven "Waterfall" approach, there is limited flexibility to move funds around. In this approach, funds get allocated to a specific project based on its' post-analyze sizing. In large enterprises, multiple function managers or departments need to fund a single project.

The movement of funds from or to a waterfall project is considerably slow. No matter how long the project is, unless there's a change request, or unless the project gets canceled or complete, allocated funds won't change. The underlying change request process and approvals required to move funds around take a long time, even months. Moreover, the project lifecycle in this approach is too long. Often, by the time the project gets complete, business needs or expected benefits are no longer relevant.

In the early 2000s, when many enterprises moved away from the traditional management approach and adopted the agile methodology, teams started to get funded for the entire year. This brought in some stability to teams for funding and resourcing. However, it didn't solve the problem of their work not being aligned to the enterprise's strategy and vision.

In some organizations, standalone agile teams are funded for the entire year based on their one-time, annual planning. During the year, teams iterate on the initiatives or features based on their roadmap, however, have no visibility if their roadmap aligns with the enterprise's strategy, vision, or objectives. Many teams operate in their silos. In this model, team leaders estimate their team's headcount or the number of people they might need to deliver the product roadmap at the beginning of the year. Funding, once allocated, does not usually move around.

After a decade, other lean-agile frameworks emerged, including SAFe (Scaled Agile Framework). SAFe does not recommend individual projects or teams to be funded but requires funding to be allocated to <u>value streams</u> within large enterprises. As described by SAFe, **value streams** represent a series of steps used to provide continuous value to a customer.

Funding value streams had many benefits over funding individual projects and teams. It led to **better visibility** of large initiatives and greater autonomy to scaled agile trains.

Do 'scaled agile' or other similar frameworks provide Funding Agility? Let's take an example. An enterprise has a total budget of 25 million and allocates 5 million to its marketing value stream, 10 million to its product development value stream, and another 10 million to its servicing value stream at the start of the year. After two months, its competitor announces a similar product at a cheaper price. How much flexibility does an enterprise have with its funds to deal with this situation? Can it quickly move funds from one funded value stream to another?

OKRs and Funding Agility

The OKR model prescribes quarterly definition and review of objectives and key results. When the OKR model is applied, **value streams can realign** their objectives every quarter, adjust their priorities, and move funds accordingly. With OKRs, objectives get aligned across the enterprise, irrespective of whether they are driven top-down or bottom-up.

With OKRs, enterprises have more Funding Agility. The quarterly definition of OKRs creates a good balance between **funding stability** and **Funding Agility**. The value streams, departments, or teams are still funded, but quarterly.

The key results (KRs) against the quarterly objectives are measured and tracked regularly, sometimes weekly or daily. When a KR is not performing well, or in other words, if there's not enough progress on the initiative or feature that contributes to a specific OKR, the value stream or a standalone agile team decides to either change course to achieve the specific OKR or abandon the same. If they decide to abandon an OKR or de-prioritize features associated with a specific OKR, they can move funds and resources to other prioritized OKRs and associated features.

The OKR model provides an opportunity for the value streams, departments, or teams to realign their priorities with that of the enterprise. It also allows personal, team-specific, and other bottom-up OKRs to be aligned with senior leaders. This Planning Agility allows funds to move around.

Summary

This chapter introduced the concept of Funding Agility to you. You now have an initial understanding of how the OKR model leads enterprises to the Funding Agility they need. In the next chapter, we will discuss the fundamentals and importance of Team Agility.

Exercise 1: Test your knowledge

- What is Funding Agility?

- Why do enterprises fail to achieve Funding Agility?

- How can OKRs support Funding Agility?

Exercise 2: Brainstorming

- Brainstorm with your team and write down 3 actions that you would take to ensure a balance between the funding stability of a team and the funding agility of an enterprise?

You may use the space below to jot down your thoughts on the exercises above.

Chapter 5 – Team Agility

Agile methods derive much of their agility by relying on the tacit knowledge embodied in the team, rather than writing the knowledge down in plans.

- *Barry Boehm*

What is Team Agility?

A team is said to be "**truly agile**" when it embraces agile principles, has an agile mindset, trusts each other, has a sustainable pace, is self-organizing, is high-performing, has a clear product roadmap, and delivers high-quality business value at a predictable velocity.

Team Agility is the ability of a team to operate with agile principles and practices. Such teams collaborate closely with the product stakeholders, are accountable for their work, adjust quickly to changing business needs, feel empowered to make decisions, and have all the skills needed to deliver value in short iterations.

For a refresher on agile and lean methodologies, refer to my published book, **The Basics Of Agile and Lean** *on Amazon: https://www.amazon.com/dp/B07P7T78XZ*

13 Steps to Improve Team Agility

Let's discuss the core characteristics that make a team "truly agile". If you desire a mature agile team, you need to focus your efforts on these thirteen aspects that lead to Team Agility.

Team culture

The culture of a team plays an important part in its agility. An agile team is open to collaborating with both internal and external teams. They work very closely with the product manager or the product owner. The team embraces an open environment built on **trust**, **respect**, and **transparency**. Such a team feels accountable for their actions and the work assigned to them. They are willing to learn from their mistakes. Most importantly, they embrace change.

Each person on a team has a responsibility and a role and knowing the value of each individual and what they bring to the table is something very special and unique.
- Hilary Knight

Clear vision, purpose, and roadmap

An agile team seeks clarity on product vision, purpose, and roadmap. They need to understand why they are doing what they are doing. An agile team operates with maximum efficiency when they are inspired by the objectives or the purpose of their work.

"Clarity of vision creates clarity of priorities."
- John C. Maxwell

The **OKR model** enhances Team Agility by providing a clear definition of objectives and key results. This, in turn, guides the product team to **align priorities** and create a product roadmap. Upon clear definition and alignment of priorities and roadmap, the agile team can focus on technical excellence and value delivery.

DevOps maturity

Agile teams need to have a flexible and scalable infrastructure to deliver value to customers more quickly. The integrated strategy between development and operations teams, advanced practices, automation tools, and the collaborative culture to quickly deliver greater value to your customers is known as '**DevOps**'.

Today, several **open-source tools** such as Git, Subversion, Jenkins, Nexus, Artifactory, etc., and cloud platforms, public or private, provide a variety of virtualized infrastructure options with real-time visibility into all stages of the development lifecycle, continuous integration, and continuous deployment.

Agile teams standardize their development and deployment tools to ensure consistency, scalability, and increased collaboration with other teams.

"True agility means that teams are constantly working to evolve their processes to deal with the particular obstacles they are facing at any given time."

- Jez Humble

DevOps provides an excellent opportunity to enforce code quality and encourage best practices. A mature DevOps strategy creates a collaborative environment that enhances the business, team, and technical agility.

Sustainable pace

Agile teams operate in short, time-boxed iterations at a sustainable pace. They deliver business value at a pace that they can sustain indefinitely without overburdening themselves. An over-worked team accumulates technical debt in the system.

"It does not matter how slowly you go as long as you do not stop."
– Confucius

The sustainable pace is not about going slow. It is finding the right balance between work and rest so that the team can continue to deliver quality work without getting burned out.

If a runner runs too fast, he or she will need to stop to catch his or her breath. On the contrary, if a runner runs at a sustainable pace, he or she can cross the finish line without stopping on the track.

Self-organization
Agile teams are mature self-organizing teams who can freely assign work to themselves, make decisions, collaborate with other teams, resolve dependencies, and remove temporary blockers on their own.

"A self-organizing team has authority over its work and the process it uses."
- Mike Cohn

Teams with high agile maturity have leaders who decentralize decision-making to reduce delays and make quick decisions. Decisions that are frequent, time-critical, or that require local context and detailed know-how should be decentralized.

If engineers are free to make decisions, they tend to be more accountable, innovative, and collaborative. Such an environment is best suited for emergent design and iterative development.

Response to change
Being responsive to change is the core attribute of a mature agile team. An agile team embraces

change and iteratively develops product features that add business value.

"Intelligence is the ability to adapt to change."
　　　　　　　　　– Stephen Hawking

Since work is organized into short, time-boxed iterations, any rework required on the work completed in past iterations is minimal.

Experimentation and discovery
Another significant attribute of a mature agile team is the continuous strive towards research, experimentation, and innovation. The agile team must be inspired to take risks, experiment with new methods, and find new solutions. This creativity lays a strong foundation for teams to adapt to changing business conditions or emerging technology trends.

"Innovation is key. Only those who will have the agility to change with the market and innovate quickly will survive."
　　　　　　　　- Robert Kiyosaki

User research, testing, and design
User research is a technique that focuses on understanding users' characteristics, pain points, activities, and behaviors to better design products or services geared towards them. In this method, the user experience team conducts a few user interviews and creates primary and secondary **personas** that represent the core users of the product. Agile teams prioritize user research such that they can build and deliver features that are most valuable to the primary product personas.

"Design used to be the seasoning you'd sprinkle on for taste; now it's the flour you need at the start of the recipe."
- John Maeda

Usability testing is a method used in user-focused product design to evaluate a product by letting a small group of users use the prototype or the product. This technique gives an understanding of how real users interact with the product or system. The primary purpose of user research and testing is to **improve the product design** such that it fulfills the needs of its users.

"Design isn't finished until somebody is using it."
- Brenda Laurel

Both user research and user testing are integral parts of user experience (UX) design that provides meaningful and relevant experience to users.

Effective facilitation

Effective facilitation of team meetings or ceremonies to refine business needs, plan work, inspect, adapt, and learn plays an important part in Team Agility. The team facilitator removes impediments, coaches the team to learn from their mistakes, and drives them towards continuous improvement.

Team structure and stability

Having a cross-functional team with high technical and domain expertise plays an important role in improving Team Agility. The members of the mature agile team respect and trust each other.

For a newly formed team, this is not a simple task. They must experience different stages of the <u>forming-storming-norming-performing</u> performance model to improve their interpersonal relationships and function as a high-performing team. This model was proposed by Bruce Tuckman in 1965. In the **'forming'** stage, most team members are positive and excited to work together. Some could feel anxious as they start to know more about their colleagues. The next stage is **'storming'** where colleagues realize differences in their working styles and feel overwhelmed or stressed. Most teams fail in this stage. In the **'norming'** stage, people start to respect their colleagues, appreciate their skills, and resolve differences with them. The **'performing'** stage is the most rewarding stage when the team starts to deliver high-quality results without much conflict. This is the desired state for high Team Agility. There's another state, **'adjourning'** which is not relevant for the agile methodology.

"Coming together is a beginning, staying together is progress, and working together is a success."
- Henry Ford

Team size is another important factor in building high-performing and stable teams. If a team is large, people tend to break down into sub-teams, experience 'social loafing', and perform worse. The optimal team size for scrum teams is around 5-9 people.

Strong partnership with customer

It is important to have a <u>customer-first mindset</u> for any team to be 'truly' agile. The agile principle, "<u>*Our highest priority is to satisfy the customer through early and continuous delivery of valuable software.*</u>" is mainly focused on satisfying the customer.

The other agile principles, "<u>*Welcome changing requirements, even late in development. Agile processes harness change for the customer's competitive advantage.*</u>" and "<u>*Business people and developers must work together daily throughout the project.*</u>" are also customer-focused.

"Don't find customers for your products, find products for your customers."
- Seth Godin

Continuous learning

Continuous learning plays an important role in a team's agility. Agile teams regularly inspect their work and adjust their behaviors to improve continuously with each iteration.

Besides product features and process improvements, mature agile teams also seek to refine the technical architecture and build an architectural runway for their emergent and simplified designs to provide maximum business value.

"Continuous improvement is better than delayed perfection."
- Mark Twain

Leadership support

Support from enterprise leaders is essential for any team to be agile. Team Agility is directly proportionate to Leadership Agility. The better the clarity a team has on its objectives, goals, and priorities, the better their motivation and performance are. Leaders can support their agile teams in different ways, including but not limited to:

- Defining a shared vision
- Aligning teams' priorities
- Creating an open environment of trust and collaboration
- Encouraging innovation and research
- Being a change agent
- Supporting teams to fail fast
- Resolving conflicts

- Inspiring people
- Empowering teams

"A leader is one who knows the way, goes the way, and shows the way."
- John C. Maxwell

OKRs and Team Agility

The OKR model provides a **common purpose** to the agile team. Team or product-level objectives, when mapped to the enterprise-level or corporate objectives, inspire the team to understand WHY they are doing what they are doing, collaborate effectively with each other, adopt an **agile mindset**, and perform their best to achieve a **shared goal**.

To understand and embrace an Agile mindset, read my article on Medium:

https://medium.com/@authoraditiagarwal/what-are-the-agile-principles-3e4d3ae0b227

Summary

Team Agility is one of the six pillars of Enterprise Agility. In this chapter, you learned the significant drivers that enhance Team Agility as summarized below:

- Team culture
- Clear vision, purpose, and roadmap
- DevOps maturity
- Sustainable pace
- Self-organization
- Response to change
- Experimentation and discovery
- User research, testing, and design
- Effective facilitation
- Team structure and stability
- Strong partnership with customer
- Continuous learning
- Leadership support

Exercise 1: Test your knowledge

- What is Team Agility?

- What factors influence Team Agility?

Exercise 2: Brainstorming

Brainstorm factors that contribute to Team Agility for your team.

You may use the space below to jot down your thoughts on the exercises above.

Chapter 6 – Technical Agility

"Any fool can write code that a computer can understand. Good programmers write code that humans can understand."
- *Martin Fowler*

What is Technical Agility?

Technical Agility for an enterprise means an ability for an enterprise to adapt to new technologies, tools, and platforms and continuously deliver high-quality technical solutions that serve the needs of their customers better. Technical Agility ensures systems or solutions developed by agile teams are robust, scalable, maintainable, secure, and architecturally sound with high quality, simple designs, best performance, and high availability.

10 Elements of Technical Agility

The core elements that contribute to the technical agility of an enterprise, program, or team are listed in the below section.

Automated unit testing

Unit testing is testing of the individual or isolated code components that allows developers to identify as many problems as possible early in the development. Defects that are found early in the development are much easier to fix.

Automation of test scripts is a critical factor in driving Enterprise Agility. Since agile development focuses on iteratively building high-quality products, it is important to automate unit tests, also called developer tests, to avoid manual errors and to identify defects early on during the development. Automated tests provide developers early feedback on the quality of the written code.

Engineers write and automate test scripts for their components using a test framework that best suits their tech stack. Many **test**

automation frameworks are available today. Some of them are listed below:

- Junit - an open-source unit testing framework which is specially designed for the Java programming language

- Jest - an open JavaScript testing library from Facebook, designed to test JavaScript libraries such as React

- BackstopJS - another simple tool to visually compare screenshots

- Enzyme - a unit testing utility specially designed to test React components

Some of the unit testing frameworks are NUnit, JUnit, Jest, Mocha, Enzyme, PhantomJS, Jasmine, Selenium Web driver, Powermock, Mockito, JTest, TestNG, Spock, and more.

Test-driven development (TDD)
The test-driven development (TDD) technique focuses on converting business needs into unit tests and then writing enough code to pass the specified test cases. In this technique, when a test is first written and executed, it fails as expected. Then, developers write the minimum amount of code required to pass the test.

Developers also ensure that code follows the rule of "**simple design**" such that it does not contain duplication or unused code, is verified by automated tests, and has minimum components or lines of code.

Since unit tests are written from the developer's perspective, this technique is also referred to as the "**inside-out**" approach. Though the initial development effort increases to some extent, the overhead is usually offset by the low defect rate and better code quality.

Acceptance tests driven development (ATDD)

ATDD, also referred to as Story Test Driven Development (SDD), is a technique that is based on TDD. In this technique, tests are automated and written upfront in a **non-technical language** based on the acceptance criteria for a story. It ensures that the acceptance criteria are known for a user story before any code is written for the same. These tests assist developers to write unit tests and develop enough code that meets the acceptance criteria for a specific user story.

Some of the common tools for ATDD are Gherkin, Cucumber, Easy, JDave, Concordion, JBehave, BeanSpec, FitNesse, and more.

"Programs must be written for people to read, and only incidentally for machines to execute."
- Harold Abelson

Behavior-driven development (BDD)
BDD, an extension of TDD and ATDD, is another technique where automated tests are written upfront in a **non-technical language** based on the conversations, real-life examples, and product behavior discussed with the team. It promotes a shared understanding between team members, before developing the code, helping them to work towards a common goal.

This technique focuses on the "**outside-in**" perspective as we are writing tests for behaviors that drive business outcomes.

"The most important property of a program is whether it accomplishes the intention of its user."
- C.A.R. Hoare

One of the core differences between ATDD and BDD is that ATDD focuses on automated tests based on acceptance criteria which fail when run until there is enough code written to pass the acceptance criteria tests, whereas BDD focuses on automated tests based on conversations on product behavior which also fail when run until enough code is written to deliver the desired behavior.

Some of the common tools for BDD are TestNG, Cucumber, Concordion, JBehave, EasyB, WebDriver.io, FitNesse, and more.

Lean UX
Lean UX is an approach to designing user experiences that users want. It is built on the solid foundation of user experience design, design thinking, agile, and lean principles. This user-centered and data-driven approach promotes continuous improvement and experimentation to evolve product design that delivers business outcomes.

The Lean UX approach starts with a benefit hypothesis. The agile team then implements and tests the hypothesis, thereby measuring and comparing the actual business outcomes or benefits with expected outcomes.

"Instead of thinking of a product as a series of features to be built, Lean UX looks at a product as a set of hypotheses

to be validated. In other words, we don't assume that we know what the user wants."
- Laura Klein

Agile teams must have **Technical Agility** to develop a high-quality and scalable solution iteratively based on **evolving product design**.

Simple design

This is another practice commonly used by agile teams that have Technical Agility. The first principle of this practice is to defer design decisions until the **last responsible moment (LRM)** to avoid any premature decisions and possible rework. The idea is to delay design decisions and keep the design options open until the cost of not making a decision becomes greater than the cost of making a decision.

The second principle is following the rules of **code simplicity**. The code is simple when there is no duplication when each idea or responsibility is expressed separately, when it is verified with the automated unit tests, and when there is **just enough code** written to pass the automated tests.

"It is not the language that makes programs appear simple. It is the programmer that makes the language appear simple!"
   - Robert C Martin

The third principle is about design patterns and other design elements. Mature teams with high technical agility encourage design patterns that promote ways to isolate variability and foster separation of concerns such as the open-closed principle that states *'software entities (classes, modules, functions, etc.) should be open for extension, but closed for modification'* or single responsibility principle that states *'every module, class, or function should have responsibility for a single part of the functionality provided by the software, and that responsibility should be entirely encapsulated by the class'*, or other such design patterns.

The balance between emergent and intentional architecture
Let's understand the difference between the two. **Emergent architecture** evolves with every iteration whereas **intentional architecture** is the intended, planned, and

upfront architecture with extensive documentation.

If you apply the **intentional architecture** or the **big design up-front (BDUF)**, you have the same risks as that with the traditional plan-driven "waterfall" approach. This approach produces lengthy documentation that no one can ever squeeze into their heads. On the contrary, if you rely purely on the **emergent architecture**, then there's be some rework and refactoring along the way.

With **emergent architecture**, an agile team delivers working software iteratively based on a technical design that evolves every iteration. The emergent architecture is based on the **'last responsible moment'** or the LRM principle (explained earlier in this book). Moreover, the emergent architecture process is to extend or enhance the architecture **only when needed** by the next set of features or business needs (also known as **'just-in-time'**).

Mature agile teams with Technical Agility maintain a **balance** between the emergent and the intentional architecture. Since **emergent architecture** could create a few problems for large organizations such as poor code quality, redundant code, delays, etc., some **intentional architecture**, upfront design, and guidelines are needed to ensure good code quality. This intentional architecture serves as the **architectural runway** which is required to create a technical foundation and a continuous flow to develop new features and capabilities. The architectural runway should be **continuously refined and extended**.

Technical Agility requires **continuous attention** to **architecture** and **design**.

Technical debt management
As quoted by _Ward Cunningham_ in 1992:

"Shipping first-time code is like going into debt. A little debt speeds development so long as it is paid back promptly with a rewrite.... The danger occurs when the debt is not repaid. Every minute spent on not-quite-right code counts as interest on that debt. Entire engineering organizations can be brought to a stand-still under the debt load of an unconsolidated implementation, object-oriented or otherwise."

Then, in 2014, _Grady Booch_ stated:

"The concept of technical debt is central to understanding the forces that weigh upon systems, for it often explains where, how, and why a system is stressed. In cities, repairs on *infrastructure are often delayed and incremental changes are made rather than bold ones. So, it is again in software-intensive systems. Users suffer the consequences of capricious complexity, delayed improvements, and insufficient incremental change; the developers who evolve such systems suffer the slings and arrows of never being able to write quality code because they are always trying to catch up."*

Outdated design, insufficient automated unit tests, absence of automated testing, lack of CI/CD pipeline (continuous integration and continuous deployment pipeline), aggressive deadlines, etc. are some of the causes that lead to the **accumulation of the technical debt**.

Mature teams with high technical agility strive to minimize their technical debt. They define a strong **'definition of done'** and include any quality checks or testing that must complete before moving the user story status to 'done'. To minimize the existing technical debt, agile teams create **visibility** of the effort required to minimize the debt and work with their business sponsors to **prioritize** the same.

"Clean code is not written by following a set of rules. You don't become a software

craftsman by learning a list of heuristics. Professionalism and craftsmanship come from values that drive disciplines."
- Robert C. Martin

Continuous experimentation

Large organizations are typically risk-averse and they have structured decision-making techniques with limited room for innovation and experimentation. With increased focus and adoption of the exploration model, large organizations are re-evaluating their existing processes to adopt a hypothesis-based, iterative approach. In this approach, teams create prototypes, such as wireframes and models, to validate their ideas, seek customer feedback, learn, and iterate.

Mature agile teams create a culture of **research** and **experimentation**. Engineers with high technical agility conduct continuous experiments to prove their hypothesis or to determine the best solution. Leaders of such teams create an open environment where engineers can brainstorm, discuss their ideas freely, conduct research, create prototypes, validate, iterate, and recommend an approach or a solution.

"Innovation needs to be part of your culture. Customers are transforming faster than we are, and if we don't catch up, we're in trouble."
        - Ian Schafer

Continuous Delivery

Continuous delivery is all about delivering value to customers early and often. It is a sum of <u>continuous or iterative development, continuous integration, and continuous deployment.</u> Let's dive deeper into each of these practices.

Continuous or Iterative Development
This forms the core of Agile methodology. Agile teams organize their work in **time-boxed** iterations or sprints. The prioritized, refined, and estimated work items or user stories at the top of the product backlog are pulled into an iteration or a sprint backlog based on the average velocity and capacity of the team. The development team commits to completing the work items in the iteration backlog within the iteration. Engineers continuously strive to deliver a high-quality, potentially shippable product increment at the end of every iteration. The agile team inspects work at the end of every iteration, adapts to their customer feedback,

and **continuously iterate** on product features. As product features evolve with each iteration, teams continually work together to increase their agile maturity.

Continuous Integration (CI)
This is the software engineering practice where engineers integrate their code changes into the main or master branch of the code frequently (at least daily or even multiple times during the day). Upon code integration, automated tests trigger and uncover defects in the code. **Continuous builds** and **automated testing** allow engineers to work on the latest source code and have immediate test results.

With CI, the defects in the code are detected at an early stage. This reduces the **cost of quality**. Another important benefit of the continuous integration practice is that it enables the product to always have a **market-ready** or **potentially shippable** state.

There are several tools that enterprises can leverage for continuous integration such as:

- Jenkins *(https://jenkins.io/)*

- Travis CI *(https://github.com/travis-ci/travis-ci)*

- GitLab CI *(https://about.gitlab.com/)*

- TeamCity *(https://www.jetbrains.com/teamcity/)*

- Bamboo *(https://www.atlassian.com/software/ bamboo)*

- BuildBot *(http://buildbot.net/)*

- GoCD *(https://www.gocd.org/)*

- Buddy *(https://buddy.works/)*

- Integrity *(http://integrity.github.io/)*

Besides these, there are many other competitive tools available in the market. This is just a sample list to give you an idea of some of the tools that are out there. The complete list of CI tools is outside the scope of this book.

Continuous Deployment (CD):
This is a software engineering practice to **release** valuable software **quickly** based on demand from customers or end-users. It is also considered as an extension to continuous integration practice that targets to minimize the time taken to deploy the code to a live / production environment. It relies on the

infrastructure which enables engineers to package their code and prepare for deployment. Continuous deployment provides **Technical Agility** to an engineering team to release their code on-demand (whenever desired). The main benefit of CD is to get early feedback from real users as product features are being released incrementally.

A few sample tools that support continuous deployment are listed below for reference:

- Jenkins *(https://jenkins.io/)*

- ElectricFlow *(https://electric-cloud.com/products/electricflow/)*

- AWS CodeDeploy *(https://aws.amazon.com/codedeploy/)*

- Shippable *(https://app.shippable.com/)*

- TeamCity *(https://www.jetbrains.com/teamcity/)*

- XL Deploy *(https://xebialabs.com/products/deployment-automation-xl-deploy/)*

- BuildBot *(http://buildbot.net/)*

OKRs and Technical Agility

Objectives are written such that they are significant, inspirational, and ambitious. To achieve such objectives, engineers work together, build an architectural runway, including a continuous delivery pipeline, and follow proven engineering practices to increase their Technical Agility. Teams working to set up their infrastructure embrace tactical OKRs that map to the corporate-level OKRs to build Technical Agility or increase time-to-market.

Summary

Technical Agility is one of the six pillars of Enterprise Agility. In this chapter, you learned the significant drivers that enhance Technical Agility as summarized below:

- Automated unit testing
- Test-driven development (TDD)
- Acceptance tests driven development (ATDD)
- Behavior-driven development (BDD)
- Lean UX
- Simple Design
- The balance between emergent and intentional architecture

- Technical debt management
- Continuous experimentation
- Continuous delivery

    o Continuous or Iterative Development
    o Continuous Integration (CI)
    o Continuous Deployment (CD)

Exercise 1: Test your knowledge

- What is Technical Agility?

- What is the difference between emergent and intentional architecture?

- What is the main difference between ATDD and BDD?

Exercise 2: Brainstorming

- Schedule time with your engineers and brainstorm factors that add technical debt to your product. List down the top 3 actions to minimize technical debt.

- Brainstorm with the team and finalize the top 3 actions that you must take to increase the technical agility of the team.

You may use the space below to jot down your thoughts on the exercises above.

Chapter 7 – Leadership Agility

"Agility is fundamental to leading a team through times of change."
- Sandra E. Peterson

What is Leadership Agility?

In today's complex, turbulent, and competitive business and technology environment, leaders need to master the skills required to become more proactive, collaborative, creative, and agile. Leadership Agility is the core competency of agile leaders to make effective decisions, inspire others, bring others along, build the best team, be proactive, develop a culture of teamwork, define objectives, and contribute to strategic initiatives for the enterprise.

7 Drivers of Leadership Agility

Leaders' agility is the core reason behind the success of any enterprise or business. Some of the common drivers of Leadership Agility are listed as below:

Being a change agent
Every agile leader must be a change agent. With this fast-paced environment, leaders need to have an entrepreneurial mindset, think ahead of their generation, have technical understanding, be a visionary, challenge the status quo, accept that change is inevitable, and be prepared to embrace the change.

Elon Musk, a technology entrepreneur, investor, and engineer, is driven by a greater purpose to help mankind and create a better future. Being the founder and CEO of SpaceX, he brought his vision of commercial space flights to reality. Elon co-founded Tesla and introduced elegant electric cars to mankind. With all his numerous endeavors, he reveals his true nature as a visionary and a change agent.

"If you are not willing to risk the unusual, you will have to settle for the ordinary."
- Jim Rohn

Several CEOs and entrepreneurs have positioned themselves as "**disrupters**" or "**change agents**" to improve humanity and to change the world. **Larry Page and Sergey Brin**, founders of Google, revolutionized search and changed the way information is retrieved from the internet. **Steve Jobs**, the co-founder of Apple, the chairman of Pixar, the CEO of NeXT, was a pioneer of the micro-computing industry. Similarly, **Jeff Bezos** who is the founder, chairman, CEO, and president of Amazon.com revolutionized e-commerce products and services to make this world a better place to live in. **Bill and Melinda Gates** are change agents who promote a better quality of life for billions of people around the world. Their primary focus is to eradicate poverty and disease from this world.

If you are in a position where your work doesn't align with your team goals, or if you are a people leader for a team whose objectives don't align with the enterprise goals, challenge the status quo and be an agile change agent.

Setting a vision and inspiring others
Good business leaders understand the importance of setting a shared vision or purpose for their teams. Their vision inspires others to come together, work with extraordinary

dedication, bring out their best abilities, and march forward to fulfill the purpose.

"A great leader's courage to fulfill his vision comes from passion, not position."
- John C. Maxwell

Elon Musk's vision to minimize the world's dependency on fossil fuels, help people to embrace sustainable energy sources, or land humans on Mars inspires thousands of highly skilled people across the world. Today, many entrepreneurs, CEOs, and business leaders set a shared vision and bring the best minds together. Look around and recognize those who inspire you to be a better leader.

Creating a culture of openness, collaboration, and trust

Every agile leader must foster an open environment of trust and collaboration where people can freely discuss their ideas, experiment with their designs, collaborate, have the freedom to make mistakes, and have fun together. Such an environment is quite conducive to foster creativity, increase velocity, and deliver high-quality work.

"You need to be aware of what others are doing, applaud their efforts, acknowledge their successes, and encourage them in their pursuits. When we all help one another, everybody wins."
- Jim Stovall

People also desire their leaders or supervisors to **trust** them and give them enough **flexibility** so they can balance their personal and professional lives efficiently. For example, certain leaders don't allow their employees to work from home. In such cases, employees often come up with new excuses such as doctor's appointments, car troubles, family emergency, furniture delivery, sick kids, and so on. Such an environment is counter-productive and is not sustainable in the long term.

Decentralizing decisions
Agile leaders must understand when and which decisions they must decentralize. Decentralized decisions reduce unnecessary delays and improve the flow of work. Not all decisions can be centralized; only frequent, time-critical, and ones that need local context or detailed background should be decentralized. Other

decisions that are long-lasting and have a large impact should remain centralized.

With decentralized decisions, the team feels more empowered to make decisions. Such self-organizing and inspired teams are an asset to any enterprise.

For example, activities such as task assignment, resolution of high-severity bugs, backlog prioritization, dependencies management, etc. are frequent and time-critical, thus must be decentralized by agile leaders.

This leadership behavior is also one of the 9 SAFe (Scaled Agile Framework) principles.

Read SAFe principles: *https://www.scaledagileframework.com/safe-lean-agile-principles/*

Embracing Lean Thinking
Successful leaders embrace lean thinking and lean principles outlined by the **House of Lean** such as Kaizen (continuous improvement), respect for people, teamwork, innovation, sustainable flow, and Genchi Genbutsu (go and see).

With lean thinking, leaders understand the significance of '**inspect and adapt**' activities such as product demo and retrospectives that promote **relentless improvement**.

"It is clear that learning agility is part of any successful leader's repertoire. The willingness and ability to learn from experience not only influences the extent to which we grow as individuals but also how we are perceived by others. Ultimately, our ability to continuously learn and adapt will determine the extent to which we thrive in today's turbulent times."
- Mitchinson., A. and Morris. R., Center for Creative Leadership

Lean thinking encourages leaders to embrace core values such as **respect**, integrity, empathy, collaboration, and teamwork. Leaders challenge the status quo and propose **innovative** ideas to bring a unique perspective to the enterprise.

Lean leaders also encourage their teams to build an architectural runway and achieve a **sustainable flow** of work. The lean principle, **'Genchi Genbutsu'**, means 'Go and See'. It suggests that a leader must go to 'Gemba' or the 'actual place' where development takes place.

Embracing Agile Principles

Agile leaders embrace the values written in the Agile Manifesto and promote the 12 Agile principles across their teams.

> *Read Agile Manifesto:*
> *https://agilemanifesto.org/*

> *Read about 12 Agile Principles with my article on Medium:*
>
> *https://medium.com/@authoraditiagarwal/w hat-are-the-agile-principles-3e4d3ae0b227*

For example, to embrace the Agile Manifesto value statement, *Individuals and interactions over processes and tools*, Agile leaders eliminate unproductive, time-consuming processes and foster an open, collaborative, and fun workspace for their teams to have frequent face-to-face conversations. For distributed teams, agile leaders promote collaboration tools like Slack or Skype for Business, encourage video conversations, and connect with their teams on a regular basis.

Knowing their customers

Successful Agile leaders understand their customer priorities, problems, and pain areas. They encourage research into customers' behaviors, responsibilities, demographics, and other attributes to define user **personas** that map to their customers. Once user personas are defined, teams start to think from the customer's perspective and make informed decisions.

"You've got to start with the customer experience and work back toward the technology, not the other way around."
- Steve Jobs

A persona is a **fictional representation** of your ideal customer based on market research, customer data, and more. The core steps involved in the process of defining user personas are as follow:

- Conducting customer interviews
- Segmenting your customers
- Setting demographic information such as age, location, marital status, professional status, religion, income group, etc.
- Describing persona background
- Describing persona goals and problems
- Applying personas to your strategy

There are many good articles and blog posts on the internet regarding guidelines to create your customer persona. The purpose of this section is not to uncover effective ways to define personas. The intent is to understand the importance of user personas and customer-first thinking for Leadership Agility.

OKRs and Leadership Agility

With the OKR model, leaders have the flexibility and space to be a change agent, think differently, encourage innovation, and adapt to changing customer needs. The OKR model acts as a framework and encourages enterprise leaders to reprioritize their goals regularly. Besides, with OKRs, leaders also have visibility on how their objectives map to the corporate and teams' objectives.

Summary

Leadership Agility is one of the six pillars of Enterprise Agility. In this chapter, you learned the significant drivers that enhance Leadership Agility as summarized below:

- Being a change agent
- Setting a vision and inspiring others
- Creating a culture of openness, collaboration, and trust
- Decentralizing decisions

- Embracing Lean Thinking
- Embracing Agile Manifesto and Principles
- Knowing their customers

Exercise 1: Test your knowledge

- What is Leadership Agility?

- When should you decentralize decisions?

Exercise 2: Brainstorming

Brainstorm the specific leadership behaviors that can enhance agility for your enterprise, portfolio, or team. List down the top 3 action items that can be taken within the next month to enhance Leadership Agility.

You may use the space below to jot down your thoughts on the exercises above.

Chapter 8 – HR Agility

"When people go to work, they shouldn't have to leave their hearts at home."
-   Betty Bender

What is HR Agility?

The ability of the HR department to quickly adapt to growing hiring needs, changing employee expectations, emerging technology trends, and new professional development methods is said to be the **HR Agility**.

While enterprises have been adopting agile or lean methodologies, the HR department has not changed much over the past years. HR departments, still, rely on **annual** performance evaluations and feedback. This creates a huge gap between the HR department and other parts of the enterprise that have adopted agile principles and are delivering value to end-users in **short**, time-boxed **iterations**.

The existing process of determining compensation and incentives for an individual is solely based on her performance during the current year which is <u>not in synergy</u> with agile principles of collaboration and teamwork. With agile, individuals help each other to deliver the highest possible value to end-users or customers. In the existing HR model where processes reward **individual contribution**, colleagues will instinctively hold back information from their peers and will find opportunities to prove themselves better than others in the team. This violates the agile principles of **trust and collaboration**.

"In order to build a rewarding employee experience, you need to understand what matters most to your people."
- Julie Bevacqua

Most enterprises adhere to an annual performance evaluation that requires **formal feedback** to be communicated to employees once or twice a year. This HR practice of mid-yearly or yearly feedback does not contribute enough to the colleague's growth and continuous development. Where, on one hand, agile teams adapt to the fast-paced and rapidly changing environment, thereby delivering valuable products with each iteration and reflecting regularly, on the other hand, HR practices are slow with feedback given half-yearly or yearly.

6 steps that HR can take to embrace agility

- Collaborate with other teams
- Separate OKRs and compensation
- Continuous feedback mechanism
- Introduce team incentives
- Introduce role agility
- Set-up HR retrospectives

Collaborate with other teams

The HR team needs to collaborate with other teams in the enterprise and understand their work environment, culture, and principles. The HR team may choose to study the work culture of other organizations as well. Secondly, the HR team can plan to 'go and see' and spend time with their colleagues across the enterprise to embrace agile principles into their everyday work. This exercise will encourage them to:

- Understand how agile teams in their enterprise operate every day
- Embrace agile principles
- Evaluate existing HR processes

Separate OKRs and compensation
OKR is not a performance evaluation tool. The performance review for an employee should not be entirely based on the OKRs. The OKR model can provide inputs into the performance evaluation of an individual.

If performance and compensation are directly tied to OKRs, behaviors that lead to _sandbagging OKRs_ are encouraged. In such conditions, teams tend to commit to simple objectives and avoid ambitious goals.

Continuous feedback mechanism
The existing process of providing semi-annual or annual feedback to employees does not align with the fast-paced agile development. The HR team should roll out **directives** and processes to ensure that a **continuous feedback** mechanism is put in place across the enterprise. Each enterprise leader should be **held accountable** to provide continuous feedback to her direct reports.

This practice will provide a continuous inspiration to colleagues as they look forward to hearing honest and candid feedback from their leaders every week, every two weeks, or every month. It will also minimize any misinterpretations, assumptions, or communication gaps between leaders and individual contributors.

With continuous feedback, colleague engagement will increase which will further reduce dissatisfaction and attrition.

Introduce team incentives
This is another **radical change** that the HR department should investigate and bring to the enterprise. Currently, there's no concept of team-wise incentives or awards given to individuals that are determined based on the overall team's achievements.

With Enterprise Agility and OKRs, there's a need for individuals to collaborate more closely and win together as a team. This doesn't align with the existing HR practice of calculating incentives or performance-based pay for individuals. Today, most enterprises award their employees based on their performance rather than based on their team's achievements.

The HR team should review their existing policies and consider incentives based on collective performance by a specific team, a business unit, or the entire enterprise _in addition to_ individual performance.

This will inspire colleagues to collaborate more, stay connected with their team's objectives, remove impediments faster, and deliver continuous business value to their customers.

Introduce role agility
The Agile methodology requires teams to be cross-functional. An engineer should be able to wear multiple hats and switch roles, as needed. For example, a front-end developer may need to switch roles and become a python engineer, or vice versa. Similarly, a UX designer may be required to develop UI components and act as a UI developer, if the need arises.

The current HR processes have no flexibility to switch roles easily. The compensation is directly tied to an individual's role in the organization.

The HR department should re-assess their practices and introduce **role agility** where individuals can easily take on additional or new roles, whenever required and get compensated for the same.

Set-up HR retrospectives

Agile retrospectives are very powerful in driving continuous improvement. With retrospectives, an agile team comes together and discusses what went well over the past week or two weeks (based on the sprint length), what could have been better, and discusses actions that should be taken to improve their existing processes.

The HR organization should adopt an agile mindset and conduct regular retrospectives like the rest of their organization. This will provide them a framework to iterate and improve relentlessly. HR retrospectives, when published, will also provide the required visibility of HR operations to other leaders of the enterprise.

OKRs and HR Agility

The HR department should embrace the OKR model the same way as other portfolios and teams across the enterprise do. With quarterly objectives, key results, and an agile mindset, the HR team can bring significant changes to their traditional practices.

The OKR model will encourage them to break their silos and communicate HR initiatives to the enterprise every quarter. With OKRs, they can measure progress against each of their objectives per quarter and set an example for other such internal departments such as Finance, Legal, Compliance, Sales, Marketing, and others.

"An organization can only be as agile as its least agile division!"
- Evan Leybourn

With increased agility in all departments, the outcomes will improve for the whole enterprise. An enterprise is truly agile only when all internal departments embrace an agile mindset and strive towards continuous growth.

Summary

HR Agility is one of the six pillars of Enterprise Agility. In this chapter, you learned the significant drivers that enhance HR Agility as summarized below:

- Collaborate with other teams
- Separate OKRs and compensation
- Continuous feedback mechanism
- Introduce team incentives
- Introduce role agility
- Set-up HR retrospectives

Exercise 1: Test your knowledge

- What is HR Agility?

- Why do you need team incentives in addition to individual incentives?

Exercise 2: Brainstorming

Brainstorm actions that your HR team should take to embrace agility. Then, narrow down to the top 3 actions and discuss them with your leader.

You may use the space below to jot down your thoughts on the exercises above.

Bibliography

Ocamb, Scott. "What does the Agile Manifesto Mean?." Scrum Alliance. 24 Apr 2013
https://www.scrumalliance.org/community/articles/2013/2013-april/what-does-the-agile-manifesto-mean

Agility Health. Enterprise Business Agility. 2019
https://agilityhealthradar.com/

Roman, Dan. "Enterprise Agility". 2019.
https://businessagility.institute/learn/enterprise-agility/

Scaled Agile. "SAFe for Lean Enterprises". Scaled Agile Inc. 2019.
https://www.scaledagileframework.com/

Pichler, Roman. "The Go Product Roadmap".
https://www.romanpichler.com/tools/the-go-product-roadmap/

About Me

Aditi Agarwal provides Agile coaching to help teams develop complex products effectively. Being a Certified SAFe Program Consultant (SPC), Certified Scrum Master (CSM), and Certified Project Management Professional (PMP), she has a proven track record of delivering high-value products and services. She is very excited to share her knowledge with her readers. Her mission is to spread knowledge, positivity, love, and compassion in the world.

Aditi lives in Phoenix, AZ with her loving family. Aditi writes short books in a straightforward and easy-to-understand language such that readers can derive maximum value without investing their time in reading bulky books.

More Books by the Author

1. _The Basics Of Agile and Lean: Develop an Agile Mindset and Lean Thinking_

   This book is written to introduce you to the core values and principles of both **Agile** and **Lean** methodologies.

   Global link: mybook.to/AgileandLean-Paperback

   Buy Now: amazon.com/dp/108124741X

2. _The Basics Of SCRUM: A Simple Handbook to the Most Popular Agile Scrum Framework_

   This book explains the **Scrum** roles, artifacts, ceremonies, and principles, along with advanced concepts such as managing technical debt, writing good user stories, publishing scrum charts, *and more. The Basics Of Scrum will be useful to those who want to learn Scrum and expand their career opportunities, or those who don't have time to read bulky books and thus need a simple reference book on Scrum.*

Global link:
mybook.to/TheBasicsOfScrum-PB

Buy Now: amazon.com/dp/1521275041

3. *The Basics Of Kanban: A Popular Lean Framework*

*This book is written to provide you with a complete reference guide on **Kanban**. Learn how to effectively manage your personal and professional work with the Lean Kanban framework.*

Global link:
mybook.to/TheBasicsOfKanban-PB

Buy Now: amazon.com/dp/1729181430

4. *An Expert Guide to Problem Solving –*
   With Practical Examples

   This book will give you an understanding of the different problem-solving tools such as **Fishbone Diagram, Brainstorming, Failure Modes and Effects Analysis, SWOT matrix, and 5Whys** *along with practical examples and applications of these tools.*

   Global link:
   mybook.to/problem-solving-pb

   Buy Now: amazon.com/dp/1539694127

5. *Emerging Technology Trends:*
   Frequently Asked Questions

   This book covers frequently asked questions about emerging technology trends such as **Blockchain, Bitcoin, Ethereum, Ripple, Artificial Intelligence, Machine Learning, Artificial Neural Networks, Deep Learning, Augmented Reality, Connected Homes, Quantum Computing,** *and more.*

Global link:
mybook.to/EmergingTrends-PB

Buy More: amazon.com/dp/1980821291

6. *Harness The Power Within: Unleash your Inner Strength with Faith, Patience, and a Positive Mind*

   The purpose of this book is to inspire you to live a happy and a fulfilled life. You can overcome any obstacle in life by unlocking the powers contained within you. There's a famous quote, "We are never defeated unless we give up on God."

   Global link:
   mybook.to/HarnessPowerWithin-PB

   Buy Now: amazon.com/dp/1544783825

7. *Embrace Positivity: Think, Speak, And Act – A 3-Step Strategy to Live Your Best Life*

   *This motivational **self-help** book reveals a 3-step strategy to embrace*

positivity *in life. It emphasizes the role of positive thinking, affirmations or the spoken word, and positive actions in attaining self-esteem and success. This book can be used as a handbook or a reference book to achieve success through a positive mental attitude.*

Global link:
mybook.to/EmbracePositivity-PB

Buy Now: amazon.com/dp/1659810566

Post your review

Your **review** will help me to improve the quality of this book and reach a wider audience. Please <u>submit your **honest review** on Amazon</u>.

Special thanks for your encouragement and continued support.

Check out my website:
https://authoraditiagarwal.com

Made in United States
Orlando, FL
30 January 2022